ACCOUNTING

HISTORY AND THOUGHT

EDITED BY
RICHARD P. BRIEF
New York University

A GARLAND SERIES

ACCOUNTING

HISTORY AND THOUGHT

EDITED BY
RICHARD P. BRIEF
New York University

A GARLAND SERIES

A HALF CENTURY OF ACCOUNTING
THE STORY OF F. W. LAFRENTZ & CO.

GARLAND PUBLISHING, INC.
New York & London
1989

Library of Congress Cataloguing-in-Publication Data

A half century of accounting, 1899-1949: the story of F.W. Lafrentz & Co.
p. cm. — (Accounting history and thought)
ISBN 0-8240-3611-5 (alk. paper)
1. F.W. Lafrentz & Co. —History. 2. Accounting firms — United States — History.
3. Accountants — United States — Biography.
I. Series.
HF5616.U7F225   1990
338.7'61657'0973—dc20   90-2759

Printed on acid-free 250-year-life paper

Manufactured in the United States of America

A Half Century of Accounting

1899-1949

The story of

F. W. LAFRENTZ & CO.

Ferdinand William Lafrentz

A Half Century of Accounting

1899-1949

PRIVATELY PRINTED FOR

F. W. LAFRENTZ & CO.

M Y ASSOCIATES have been gracious indeed in dedicating this volume to me. I must hasten to point out that the achievements of which the story tells are not mine alone; rather they are the product of cooperation, friendship and understanding — which have been a part of our organization since its founding fifty years ago.

"Cruelly sweet are the echoes that start when memory plays an old tune on the heart" — and the story told here brings to mind many an incident which had grown obscure with time.

It shows, too, I think, what can be accomplished in this great country under our free enterprise system. Some there are who believe that opportunity today is limited; I do not agree. The "land of the free and the home of the brave" is no idle phrase to me; it has never been since I first set foot on these hospitable shores seventy-six years ago. There are still frontiers for those willing to bestow on the least things the same effort and care they bestow on the greatest.

I am sure that the men of F. W. Lafrentz & Co. will continue to advance the cause of the accounting profession in the years to come. I am grateful to them for what they have done and what I know they will do; and I salute them and wish them well.

F. W. Lafrentz

The New York State Society of Certified Public Accountants

as it celebrates the Fiftieth Anniversary of the founding of the Society, desires to do honor to

Ferdinand William Lafrentz

the only surviving member of the Society who has held his certificate from the State of New York as a Certified Public Accountant for over Fifty Years; Therefore, be it

Resolved, by the Board of Directors on behalf of the Society, that we extend our congratulations to

Ferdinand William Lafrentz

on this

Golden Anniversary

and that we express our sincere and heartfelt appreciation of his services to this Society, to the profession and to the community which he has served for over a half-century– as Teacher, as Poet, as Public Servant, as Philanthropist, as a distinguished Practitioner of his Profession on the highest levels of competency and integrity, as President of the American Association of Public Accountants, as Vice-President and Director of the New York State Society of Certified Public Accountants and as Chairman of the New York State Board of Certified Public Accountant Examiners;

Fully realizing, as we do, that the history of our Profession and of our Society for this first half century would not be complete without this recognition of his great contribution to their advancement and development.

April 21, 1947

A testimonial presented to F. W. Lafrentz by the New York State Society of Certified Public Accountants on the commemoration of its Fiftieth Anniversary.

THE PLACE: U.S.A.—THE TIME: 1899

THE YEAR 1899 was a year of action. The United States acquired the Philippine Islands. The flag was raised over the Island of Guam. There was a great parade in New York City for Admiral Dewey.

A universal peace conference was proposed by the Czar of Russia, and the permanent Court of Arbitration was established at the Hague. We signed a treaty of commercial reciprocity with France, and agreed with England on a temporary boundary for Alaska. In the White House, William McKinley was President.

Rushing zestfully ahead, a growing giant, the United States was not quite certain of the future. But there were many who felt certain its destiny was one of greatness. The financial panic of 1893 was now just a memory, and America was the land of hope and promise.

To all who sought freedom, and opportunity, our shores signalled welcome. More than three hundred thousand immigrants arrived that year, each seeking a better life, each with faith in the country's future and with hope for his own. The United States seemed a new western frontier for the old world.

One of those who watched the tide of immigration with more than casual interest was Ferdinand William Lafrentz. He, too, had immigrated to the United States. But that had been twenty six years before, and he could testify to the problems and the opportunity these new Americans would face.

Now he was 40 years old. He had made his mark in three fields — law, finance and accounting. He was ready to start a new phase of his career.

What he did was to found The American Audit Company, the predecessor of the accounting partnership which bears his name, F. W. Lafrentz and Co.

F. W. Lafrentz — *front row center* — with a few of his students, in 1881, at Bryant & Stratton Business College, where he was head of the Practical Business Department.

FERDINAND WILLIAM LAFRENTZ

L IKE MOST OF THOSE who came to the United States during the great flood tide of immigration, Ferdinand William Lafrentz sought opportunity which did not exist in his native land.

He had been born in 1859, of German parents, on the Island of Fehmarn, then a part of Denmark. The boy was six when an important event occurred: Germany annexed Schleswig-Holstein, and he became a citizen of Germany. But he was too young to be interested in that, just as he was too young to know of the great war which had engulfed the home of his future.

His schooling was good, and young Lafrentz showed an early flair for skills which were to stand him in good stead in later years. His ability to compose verse — another characteristic which has remained with him — also attracted the attention of his school-mates and teachers.

Those who were his intimates knew him for his humor, and friendliness and a kind of boyish leadership and sense of imagination. They were useful qualities in Fehmarn, and they proved very handy indeed when the boy arrived in the United States in 1873, at the age of fourteen, as confused as would be any other child who found himself suddenly, and irrevocably, in a strange country.

AN ENGAGEMENT IN CHICAGO

His first stop was Chicago. There, working in a store owned by an aunt and uncle, he began to master English and learn the ways of his new country. He wanted to learn as much as he could and, for six years his school was the store. Then, in 1879, he enrolled as a student at the Bryant and Stratton Business College. That was just about a year before he became an American citizen, on October 29, 1880, at the age of 21.

His record at the business college was good enough to win him a post as assistant professor at the Metropolitan Business College, where he stayed for a while before returning to Bryant and Stratton as assistant head of the Practical Business Department. Soon he became department head, and spread out by taking charge of classes in higher mathematics and German.

Teaching was fun, and young Lafrentz was good at it. But then as now, teaching was not a very highly paid profession. Besides, he had other, broader interests.

A turning point — though it did not necessarily seem to be then — was an invitation he received to handle an accounting assignment for a Chicago banking firm, Snydacker and Company. This engagement proved so successful all around that, in 1881, he accepted a job as an accountant with the firm.

OFF FOR THE WEST

It was then that he began to hear more about the west. For some of the Snydacker clients had cattle interests, and young Lafrentz got to know them, and got to hear about some of the things going on out in the cowboy country which he was later to celebrate in verse. The upshot was that within three years he left the banking firm to join the headquarters force of a cattle company in Wyoming. He had an office in Cheyenne; he had responsibility, too, for he was in charge of the company's financial affairs.

The ten years which followed were eventful and happy ones. While in the West he had an opportunity to study, to learn and to grow. And during this period he married Emma Louise Poole, of Brooklyn, in 1885.

In Wyoming, he became a member of the Territorial Legislature and introduced the joint resolution requesting that the territory be admitted into the Union. Wyoming entered the Union in 1890. A fellow legislator who was to become a life-long friend was Willis Van Devanter, later United States Supreme Court Justice.

About this time, Mr. Lafrentz began to give serious thought to a professional career in accounting. There was a growing need for accounting services in a country becoming more and more rapidly industrialized. He sensed that accounting would play an important part in the country's economic expansion.

Consequently, in 1889, he moved to Ogden, Utah, and set himself up in practice. His stay here was short but productive, for during the next three years he studied law and won admission to the bar on October 28, 1893.

While he was in Ogden, Henry C. Wilcox, counsel for the American Surety Company in New York and Mr. Lafrentz's best man at his wedding eight years earlier, stopped by for a short visit. Transcontinental travel was rigorous in those days, and Mr. Lafrentz prevailed upon his friend to rest up before going on to San Diego to investigate a claim against his company. In explaining the investigation that he was to make, Mr. Wilcox said he would need an accountant to help him get at the facts. Mr. Lafrentz became interested and volunteered to go along without compensation. His offer was accepted.

This proved to be the major turning point in his life, for the report he prepared on the investigation impressed the president of the American Surety Company, William Lee Trenholm. The result was an invitation to join that organization in its New York office as a claim auditor.

BACK TO THE EAST

Mr. Lafrentz agreed, and arrived in the city in 1893. He was thirty-four years old.

He looked at his new work as an opportunity for advancement. And it was. With his family settled in Brooklyn Heights, he quickly entered into his new surroundings with vigor and imagination. Within a year and a half he helped to revise the company's accounting system and adapt it to the changing needs of the times.

Mr. Lafrentz was new to New York — the center of this country's business and financial activities — but he was not unknown. And as he increased his business activity, it was not surprising that, in addition to his duties with the American Surety Company, he should find opportunities for other accounting work.

His first independent client was George C. Boldt, proprietor of the old Waldorf-Astoria Hotel, who became a fast life-long friend. Mr. Lafrentz handled his accounting as long as Boldt lived. Other business organizations soon became interested in the young accountant and offered him opportunities to help them.

By 1899, Mr. Lafrentz's personal clientele had grown to substantial proportions. He had surrounded himself with capable men who did his accounting work under his supervision. With his promotion that year to comptroller of the American Surety Company, he decided to form a company to handle his independent practice, so that he would be able to meet the demands of both his surety work and of his personal accounting clients. His own company he called The American Audit Company.

This was the beginning of a two-fold career. Blessed with a full share of energy, Mr. Lafrentz welcomed the opportunity to expand his activities in the accounting field and to continue his active work with the American Surety Company. He was to become president of American Surety in 1912 and, in 1926, Chairman of the Board.

In his role as head of The American Audit Company, he established his first offices on the Bradley-Martin Ballroom balcony at the Waldorf-Astoria, then at Fifth Avenue and 34th Street. This — in 1899 — was the origin of what was to become F. W. Lafrentz & Co. on January 1, 1923.

PROFESSIONAL INTERESTS

In the years that followed, Mr. Lafrentz played an active part in the early growth of the accounting profession. He was active in the American Association of Public Accountants and served this society in various executive capacities. He was president from 1901 to 1903. He was one of those who helped gain passage of the first CPA law in the United States, enacted by the New York State legislature in 1896. He was also among the first members of the New York State Society of Certified Public Accountants, founded in 1897.

New York University was the first college in New York State —

and the fifth college in the United States — to establish a school of commerce and accounts. Mr. Lafrentz was associated with the late Charles Waldo Haskins, a pioneer accountant and the school's first dean, in its establishment. For years he was a trustee and lecturer in the school. He was also a member of the New York State Board of CPA Examiners from 1903 to 1907 and, again, from 1917 to 1925, when he resigned the chairmanship at the age of sixty-eight. This board prepared and conducted examinations and passed on the qualifications of applicants for the CPA certificate.

A member of the same board for fifteen years, and for many years its secretary, was the late Charles S. McCulloh who became a member of the Lafrentz organization in 1923.

Through national societies, Mr. Lafrentz was active in helping to establish and maintain high professional standards. When the American Institute of Accountants came into being in 1916 — as the successor organization to the American Association of Public Accountants — he served on its first Council. He is still an ex-officio member. In 1917, the Institute adopted a code of ethics and conducted its first examinations for admission to the Institute. Through the Institute, the profession developed uniform CPA examinations which were, in time, adopted by forty-six states, the District of Columbia and the territories of Alaska, Hawaii, Puerto Rico and the Virgin Islands.

The personal story of F. W. Lafrentz has many aspects. His interests are widespread. His career in the American Surety Company alone has been a full one. But his energy kept him a part of the accounting profession. Today, at the age of ninety, he still takes an active interest in all that goes on. He and his wife celebrated their golden wedding fourteen years ago, in 1935. They have one son, Arthur F. Lafrentz, who is a partner in F. W. Lafrentz & Co., and two daughters, Miss Olga L. Lafrentz and Mrs. James T. Bryan.

As a boy Mr. Lafrentz had shown a lively flair for poetry. And despite his business responsibilities, he has continued this interest. As early as 1881 he published his first book of verse, "Nordische Klange," about his native Island of Fehmarn. Written in his native tongue, it was acclaimed. When in 1922 it was reprinted, it brought $5,000, which he gave to an institute for lung diseases he had established years before at Fehmarn.

His philanthropic interests gave rise to another book of poetry in later life. This was called "Cowboy Stuff" and covered his life in the West. It was written expressly to raise subscription funds for building the Lafrentz-Poole dormitory at Lincoln Memorial University at Cumberland Gap, Tennessee, in which he had become interested in 1924. Approximately $150,000 was realized.

The dormitory was dedicated in 1929 to his mother and his wife's mother. Mr. Lafrentz himself has served as president of the Board of Trustees and is now its chairman. He also holds the honorary degree of Doctor of Literature from the University.

December 3, 1946, was the fiftieth anniversary of the day when Mr. Lafrentz received his CPA certificate in New York State. He is the only living member of the New York State Society of Certified Public Accountants to have held his certificate so many years. To honor that occasion, his associates in the firm established the F. W. Lafrentz Gold Key and Scholarship Fund at the New York University School of Commerce and Finance. This award is made to the male evening student, majoring in accounting, who receives the highest average grades in English through his junior year. The ability to write clear and lucid prose is essential in accounting, and this is emphasized by the provisions of the scholarship award.

F. W. Lafrentz is a man who has always liked activity, and people, and friends. He is still active today, and his circle of friends is a wide one. The principles which motivated his early life still guide him.

THE EARLY YEARS

AMERICA WAS YOUNG among the nations of the world — and in a hurry. Like a growing boy, bursting at the seams, America was hard to pace. It was lusty and proud, crude and sensitive.

Business reflected the times. Its leaders were individualists. But methods of doing business were beginning to undergo change. Private ownership and completely private control were giving way increasingly to the corporate form of enterprise, and a new social consciousness of public responsibility on the part of business was arising.

The year 1899 saw a tide of immigration — labor to fill the young giant's appetite for development of its mines and factories. Railroad systems were spreading like spider webs to criss-cross the nation. Shipyards sounded with the clatter of jackhammers. The swelling population needed homes, clothes and all manner of goods. Inventions of astonishing importance were being refined. Edison's incandescent lamp and the talking machine, the electric generator and the electric motor were great new tools. For the first time the prospect of flying machines, the wireless and the automobile were more than dreams.

There was nothing simple about this great new industrial frontier. For one thing, business methods and techniques were not wholly adequate to meet the social demands of a changing economic picture. And it was here that the accounting profession came face to face with a challenge.

THE START OF A PROFESSION

The roots of accounting go back for hundreds of years. But in the United States, at the turn of the century, accounting was still the newest of the professions. Its achievements were all in the future. Its services in an ever-expanding economy were still to be demonstrated.

When F. W. Lafrentz founded The American Audit Company in 1899, the country's first law governing accounting was only three years old. The American Association of Public Accountants was twelve years old. That the Association had been founded was due mainly to the efforts of an English accountant, James T. Anyon, who was brought to this country by Edwin Guthrie to manage the accounting firm of Barrow, Wade and Guthrie. Anyon had been surprised to learn that there was no organization similar to The Institute of Chartered Accountants in England and Wales. Six weeks after arriving in the country in 1886, he gathered a few accountants together to lay the foundations for the first permanent professional society. Later he became its first secretary and played a major role in the passage of the first CPA law in New York State.

Accountants at that time were often "overworked and underpaid." Night work and Sunday overtime were routine. There were even some hesitant clients who did not wish others to know that they had employed professional accountants — for fear someone might think trouble was afoot. This provides a strange contrast with the conditions of today when — as Stuart Chase has remarked — the certificate of a CPA on a financial report is "something like the Sterling mark on silver."

These were the days of gas lights, crank-up telephones, pot bellied stoves and high stools, of the normal ten-hour day and six-day work week.

And they were days of growing pains for the accounting profession. Business, too, had its growing pains. In the years to come business and accounting were to join hands to participate in an economic expansion the like of which the world had never dreamed.

But as the Twentieth Century opened, all this was in the future.

It was a busy time, of course, for the members of the young Lafrentz organization. It was a busy time for the whole accounting profession.

One basic surge was the movement toward increased professionalism. State societies of certified public accountants began to spring up, for the purpose of protecting their members, promoting the passage of laws governing accounting in their States, and establishing standards and ethics. The accounting profession had a long way to go, but even then it was on the way.

By 1905, a dozen colleges had recognized the need for the formal teaching of accounting skills. And the passage of the New York CPA law in 1896, and the founding of the New York State Society of Certified Public Accountants the following year, had a stimulating effect on professional growth in many other parts of the country. Mr. Lafrentz was one of those who welcomed these trends and tried to speed them.

EARLY BUSINESS PROBLEMS

And there were business affairs to attend to. In 1900 — the year New York University opened its School of Commerce and Accountants, the Lafrentz organization opened its second office. It was a long way from New York — hundreds of miles away, in Atlanta.

In the following decade, six more offices were established: Boston and Chicago, in 1901; Washington, in 1903; New Orleans, in 1904; Baltimore, in 1906; and Richmond, in 1907. Some of the firm's clients were expanding into those cities. Besides, there was the need to provide accounting services for local business firms which were also expanding with the general economy.

These new offices of the firm — like many another new accounting office — were small and modest. Boston opened with two regular clients, for example, though with enough work to make members of the staff in that city regard the seven-day week as routine. There were financial problems, too, and evidence to support the saying that the bills of the accountant, like those of the doctor, were among the last to be paid.

In Richmond, the office's first engagements were for a small bank, a paper company and for a hotel.

The Washington office opened with no business on the books at all, and its first engagement was auditing the books of a real estate firm in bankruptcy. The records of the real estate firm proved to be crude, and included only "press copy" books and check books with meager cash records. There were no ledgers or journals.

In the midst of these problems, the organization found it necessary to secure representation in England, to serve clients with business interests in that country. Relationships were established with Martin, Farlow & Company, a firm of chartered accountants founded in the 1880's by James (later Sir James) Martin and Arthur R. King-Farlow.

The problems faced by the growing profession were difficult, but they were normal for the times and the customs.

For the activities of business were bubbling and expanding, and many a young accounting firm went through the experience of finding that the mushrooming growth of a client presented a real "servicing" problem. If a client with headquarters in one town suddenly opened branches or operations in two or three other cities — just how could the CPA handle that?

Sometimes accountants found themselves spending as much time "on the road" as in their offices in order to do the work that had to be done. Another solution lay in the decentralization of accounting firms. Where the client went — there went the accountant. In some cases, accountants used still a different method and arranged for professional friends to represent them in distant cities.

Coincident to the problem of meeting clients' requirements for service in various parts of the country was the internal problem of establishing uniform working papers and procedures, so that when reports were prepared and brought together, business would be able to obtain a clear picture of its operations.

Inconvenience for the accountants was the rule rather than the exception in these days. It was all just a part of the day's work.

There is a story about Arthur F. Lafrentz, son of the founder, on an occasion when he was working on the books of a New York company in its warehouse. There was only a pot-bellied stove for warmth. His "facilities" included a rickety stool and a packing case for a desk. To make matters more awkward and disconcerting, large casks were constantly being dropped on the floor above,

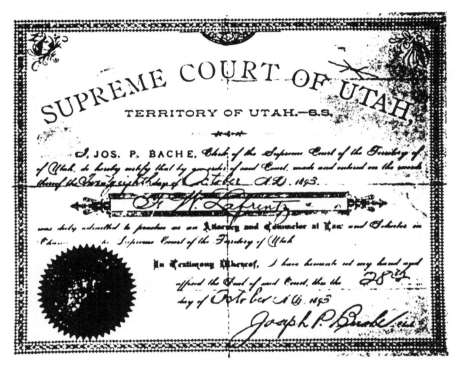

In 1889, F. W. Lafrentz moved to Ogden, Utah, and established his own accounting practice. He also studied law and was admitted to the bar on October 28, 1893.

making a great racket and covering young Lafrentz, the ledger and other records he was examining, with lumps of dirt and showers of dust from between the rafters.

But accountants were too busy to bother about discomforts and inconveniences. Business needed their services; accounting was winning a place, even though the theories of accounting were often not fully understood or appreciated.

THE TAX PROBLEM

One of the problems of the day involved the public responsibilities of the accountant. While working for his client, he had to maintain complete independence of judgment. Today — though not always then — the independence of the CPA is recognized.

An example of the leadership demonstrated by accountants during this period in the field of income tax accounting was described by George O. May in his excellent book, "Financial Accounting." * Mr. May said:

"The first modern tax levied by the Federal Government on corporate income was the Excise Tax imposed in 1909. It was a hasty political maneuver and made its appearance in the Senate as an amendment to the tariff bill. Framed by distinguished lawyers, it contemplated the measurement of income through the use of accounts of a form to which the legal mind was accustomed — a statement of receipts and disbursements — though an allowance for "depreciation" and losses was incompatibly included in the scheme. The introduction of this proposal was the occasion for one of the first organized presentations of the accounting point of view. A group of leading firms protested against the naivete and unworkability of the proposal. The Attorney-General, however, brushed aside the protest with an ironical expression of his faith in the ability of the accountants to overcome any difficulty which the law might present, and the measure was enacted substantially as originally proposed.

"The Treasury, called upon to administer the law, soon realized the justice of the criticisms that had been offered. It found it im-

* Copyright, 1943, by The Macmillan Company and used with their permission.

possible to solve the problem without, in effect, adopting the substance of the proposals that the accountants had made. After conferring with advisers, such as W. J. Filbert, comptroller of the United States Steel Corporation, and A. Lowes Dickinson, a leading practicing accountant, it adopted a regulation which provided that the term 'actually paid' used in the law did not necessarily contemplate that there should have been an actual disbursement of cash or even of its equivalent, but that under the law an item would be deemed to be paid as soon as the taxpayer recognized that it had to be paid by recording it as a liability. This artificial rule, made practically necessary by the unfortunate wording of the law, had a permanent effect on the development of our taxing system."

While the amount of the tax imposed under this law was small, passage of the statute was one of the factors which helped to enlarge the need for accounting services.

This trend was even more pronounced after the passage of the income tax law which went into effect in 1913. The *Journal of Accountancy,* in its November issue of 1913, commented that the new income tax law was to have a "far more far-reaching effect upon public accountants than upon any other profession or business in the country."

Soon this proved to be true. For the determination of income is basic in income taxation, and the determination of income — not always as easy as it might appear to the layman — is based on accounting concepts. The growing complexity of income tax laws has presented the profession with a major challenge, but at the same time it has helped to make tax work one of the accountant's principal fields of activity.

These factors which stimulated the growth of the profession also stimulated the development of the Lafrentz organization. By 1914 the firm was strongly established in eight offices. Its clientele had grown substantially, and the firm was servicing enterprises in a number of important fields, among them textile manufacturing, lumber mills, railroads, hotels, banks and public utilities.

The increase in business and the added responsibilities in accounting led automatically to the enlargement of the regional staffs. In New York, one of the men who joined the firm to help carry the load was Harry M. Rice, a pioneer of early accounting.

The specter of war in Europe began to close in on America. The remoteness of the conflict, both psychological and physical, was suddenly shattered, and the nation found itself face to face with its first major overseas war. Industry was called on to produce as never before — to meet the greatest challenge it had ever faced in the national interest. The accounting profession faced a challenge and a great opportunity for public service.

George C. Boldt, proprietor of the old Waldorf-Astoria Hotel, who was F. W. Lafrentz's first accounting client in New York.

EXPANSION: 1914 AND AFTER

THE WAR YEARS — all the events of that decade — helped to change the face of the world. The accounting profession did not escape.

During the war itself, while the facilities of business were geared for battle, business men increasingly needed accounting help. There were wartime tax problems, cost problems, auditing problems.

And then, when the war was done, new problems took the place of the old. The Revenue Acts of 1917 and 1918, for example, introduced the excess profits taxes, and again the services of accountants were in demand. The Treasury Department sought the advice of the profession, and a certified public accountant was named Deputy Commissioner of Internal Revenue, in charge of rules and regulations.

The accounting profession had won recognition. Of that there could be no doubt. But that did not mean that the future was going to be simple.

Fortunately there were clear heads to guide the profession. F. W. Lafrentz, through his efforts on the first Council of the new American Institute of Accountants, was one of scores of public spirited accountants who helped to clear the fog of indecision and lay out standards of procedure. It was a common task for all members of the profession.

Certainly it is a fitting commentary on the profession's accomplishments that its members were able to meet this problem successfully.

All phases of accounting were stimulated. Schools and colleges became aware of the new importance of accounting and adjusted their courses of study. The American Institute of Accountants took part in this development. State Boards of Examiners raised their standards of examination. The certified public accountant became recognized as a member of a skilled profession.

The young American giant for the first time was beginning to feel his strength, to know his position in the World of Nations. Almost overnight the United States became a leader instead of a hesitant and sometimes recalcitrant follower.

The accounting profession played an important part in building this strength by providing a means, a technique, for the systematic recording, analyzing and reporting of business operations — by developing a "language" which government, management, labor and investors could more readily understand in common. Accounting rapidly was becoming the language of business — a technique for measuring, evaluating and forecasting business progress.

The Lafrentz organization was a part of this scene. Arthur Lafrentz was called on to serve in Washington, where he became Chief of the Credit Section of the War Credit Board, which approved over $300,000,000 in credit advances to contractors supplying war materials under government contract. Other members of the firm also served in the Armed Forces and in capacities where they could bring the benefit of their broad business experience in the successful prosecution of the war.

Surely the period of the first World War was a milestone in the development of accounting. It was also a milestone in the development of the Lafrentz organization.

POSTWAR YEARS

This country escaped physical damage and the problems of reconstruction faced by the Allies. It did face, however, a dual task: the need for reconversion and the need for expansion of production to meet the demand for a higher standard of living.

The shock of the war had solidified the thinking of men and had shown them the possibilities of mass production and national distribution, and the creation of new wealth.

Business was cost conscious. And it was tax conscious. Business leaders realized the necessity of developing financial methods which would smooth the path ahead.

There was a short period of business recession in 1921. But the country quickly regained its balance. Then with the star of expansion bright before it, business began its hard, rapid rise. The Lafrentz organization expanded too, in order to better serve its clients moving into broader fields and to enlarge and strengthen its own organization.

Chicago, rising in importance as America's number two city, promised a boom. The Lafrentz organization's office there since April 1901 had grown with the region's economy. It was now evident that it required closer attention if the growing needs of the firm's clients were to be met. As a result, J. Arthur Marvin, who had joined the staff of the Richmond office in 1914, was transferred to Chicago as resident manager. He took over these duties in 1921.

One of the trends of the twenties which affected the accounting world was the lively public interest in investments. Capital, supplied by private individuals, by banks, by insurance companies, was the life blood of the new factories which needed tools and machines to meet the demand for consumer and capital goods.

And the new tax laws, of course, gave rise to disputes between taxpayers and the Bureau of Internal Revenue, so that accountants found themselves called on more and more to represent their clients in tax matters.

The world of the accounting profession seemed at times to have some internal, centrifugal force at work. Change, growth and expansion: these were basic characteristics.

A PARTNERSHIP IS FORMED

One effect of the rapidly changing scene was a decision on the part of the Lafrentz officers to change the firm's pattern of organization. The American Audit Company had been a corporation, conducted in accordance with the ethics of the accounting profession; but it was felt that there were advantages, in view of the firm's enlarging scope of activities and responsibilities, in changing to a partnership.

On January 1, 1923, F. W. Lafrentz and Arthur F. Lafrentz formed the partnership of F. W. Lafrentz & Co.

Harry M. Rice, who had served with The American Audit Company as a vice-president since 1913, became a partner in New York. Another who became a partner in New York was Charles S. McCulloh, who joined the firm at this time.* All resident managers were offered resident partnerships.

The firm's practice continued to grow, and it was soon felt that the basis of participation should be broadened even further. As a result, J. Arthur Marvin transferred from Chicago to New York, and on January 1, 1928, joined F. W. Lafrentz, Arthur Lafrentz, Mr. Rice and Mr. McCulloh as one of the five managing partners.

Arthur Lafrentz had continued to devote a good deal of his time to the American Surety Company, the same firm which his father had joined in 1893. In 1928 the son became first vice-president of the surety company, and six years later was elected president.

The years immediately before the great depression were busy and productive for the new partnership.

The surge of business toward the west involved some of the firm's clients, and the need for offices and bases of operation on the west coast became apparent. For some years the firm had been represented there by Bullock, Kellogg & Mitchell, and this west coast group merged its practice with F. W. Lafrentz & Co. on January 1, 1929. Offices were located in San Francisco, Oakland and Los Angeles.

A little later, representation was established in Seattle through Arne S. Hansen & Co., and in 1935 a partnership was formed with Mr. Hansen to handle the expanding activities of the firm's clients in the Pacific-Northwest.

* Charles S. McCulloh, for many years a leading member of the accounting profession, was born in Riverdale, N. Y., on July 1, 1856. After attending schools there and in New Jersey, he took his first job with an insurance company and then entered the accounting department of the Equitable Life Insurance Society. In 1881, he established his own accounting practice, and later, in 1898, joined the firm of Haskins and Sells, where he became a partner. He re-established his own firm six years after he became a partner, however, and built up a successful practice before joining the Lafrentz organization as a partner in 1923. Mr. McCulloh served on the New York State Board of CPA Examiners from 1910 until 1926, for a time as President and as Secretary. He was widely known, not only as a leading accountant but also as an active sports enthusiast. He died at 84, on December 26, 1940.

As the "Roaring Twenties" moved along, with almost no apparent sign of let-up, there were only a few who sensed the possibility of collapse. The pace seemed so swift, so free. But, the years of limitless prosperity were rushing to an end. And, one day in 1929, the lightning struck.

That year, F. W. Lafrentz & Co. was just thirty years old. It had permanent offices in New York, Boston, Baltimore, Washington, Richmond, Atlanta, New Orleans, Cleveland, Chicago, San Francisco, Los Angeles and Oakland.

The firm was now strongly established, and prepared to meet the problems that lay ahead.

Charles S. McCulloh

HOUSE
OF
REPRESENTATIVES

10TH
LEGISLATIVE
ASSEMBLY

WYOMING.

While in Cheyenne, Wyoming, F. W. Lafrentz was in charge of the financial affairs of a cattle company. He also became a member of the Territorial Legislature where be introduced the joint resolution requesting that the Territory be admitted to the Union. Wyoming was admitted to the Union in 1890.

A CHANGING ECONOMY

WHEN THE PROSPERITY BUBBLE BURST, the shock was felt throughout the World. For by this time, America's influence in international commerce had won it a top place among the nations of the World. Now, ironically, the giant lay prostrate, stunned and bewildered.

Factories stood idle. Millions read the "help wanted" columns. At the worst period, unemployment was estimated at a shocking 11,842,000. And the national income dipped from $87,355,000,000 in 1929 to a low of $39,584,000,000 in 1933.

Along with the collapse came a whole melange of laws, regulations, rules, restrictions, and confusion. The ten years between 1929 and 1939 brought about a changing social approach. Out of this period came the social security laws and Federal provisions for unemployment insurance.

The period was marked by a greatly accelerated movement toward increased regulation of business by governmental agencies. And all of this had its effect on the accounting profession.

Arthur M. Schlesinger, Sr., the Harvard historian, has written:

"The New Deal involved not only the greatest peacetime centralization of authority the country had ever known, but also a vast extension of the power of the executive at the expense of the legislative . . . soon a maze of commissions, boards and other agencies sprang up in Washington, many of them empowered to issue rules and regulations that bore the effect of law. . . ."

It was a period of bewildering change. Hope alternated with despair, as the nation struggled up out of its worst depression. It was a time of trouble, and controversy, and new ideas.

A good many of these new ideas meant problems for business. In 1933 Congress passed the National Industrial Recovery Act and the Securities Act. The following year the Securities-Exchange

Act was enacted, and in 1935 the Federal Social Security Act, The National Labor Relations (Wagner) Act, Glass-Steagall Banking Act, and the Public Utility Holding Company Act were passed.

At every turn, business was confronted with a whole maze of new problems.

And as for the accounting profession, it was almost engulfed with work. When a new law was enacted, business turned usually to its lawyers for legal advice and to the certified public accountants for accounting advice. Reclassification of accounts and re-systematizing of procedures presented many technical problems. In many cases the system of keeping records had to be reorganized. Cost accounting and methods of financial reporting had to be expanded to give more information to conform with Securities and Exchange Commission regulations.

PUBLIC SERVICE

Some of the work load which the accounting profession had to absorb was concerned wholly with the problems of clients. But there were also many opportunities for public service.

In 1930, for example, the American Institute of Accountants appointed a special committee to work with the New York Stock Exchange to study the problems of financial reporting, which were becoming more and more important because of the depression.

In 1932, the New York Stock Exchange issued a report on the study. It focused attention on the need for improving the presentation of financial reports. Principles were established and adopted by the Exchange. All listed companies were notified that these principles were to be followed in the future.

A year later the New York Stock Exchange went a step further. It outlined six points to be followed in preparing financial reports. It also required all companies listing stock on the "Big Board" to have their financial reports audited by independent auditors. Other Exchanges followed suit.

Further recognition was gained by the accounting profession with the passage of the Securities Act of 1933 and the Securities-Exchange Act of 1934. These acts gave power to the Securities and Exchange Commission to make accounting rules covering the presentation of financial statements related to public financing and with registration on the stock exchanges.

But accountants believed the initiative for the promulgation of rules and regulations, and their application, should originate within the profession. As a consequence, the American Institute of Accountants appointed a committee to cooperate with the Commission. Harmonious relations were quickly established through the office of the Chief Accountant of the S. E. C.

Recognizing the authority of the Institute and its purpose, the Commission permitted the profession to take the initiative. The Institute established its Research Department and started to issue bulletins on accounting practice and procedures and on auditing procedure. That the profession met the challenge successfully has been demonstrated in the 37 bulletins on accounting procedure and 24 statements on auditing procedure that have been issued by the Institute over the years. They are accepted by business, Government, and the accounting profession as authoritative.

Throughout the entire period of the thirties, until the country again became engulfed in war, the accounting profession continued to meet the changing needs of changing times.

For the men of the Lafrentz organization, as for the men of so many other accounting firms — the depression years were difficult, often discouraging and always arduous. But the firm was busy with its clients' affairs, and it retained all of its key personnel.

F. W. Lafrentz was one of those who helped sustain morale, and he was often likely to remind a discouraged associate or staff member of the Irishman, down on his luck, who said: "Yesterday was bad. Today is even worse. But thin we have the illigant future before us."

Another time he said: "The only place where peace, prosperity and happiness can be found is in the dictionary, and even there one is obliged to search them out."

His faith was one of the factors in the firm's high rate of activity during these troubled years. And, at the end of the decade, the firm was stronger and more firmly established.

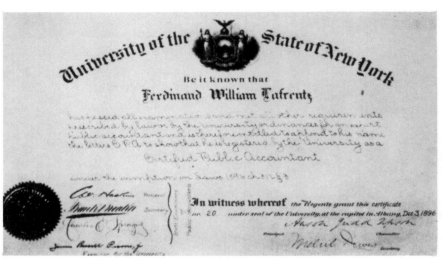

F. W. Lafrentz played an active part in the early growth of the accounting profession. He was one of those who helped gain passage of the first CPA law in the United States, enacted by the New York State legislature in 1896. He received CPA certificate Number 20 on December 3, 1896.

WORLD WAR II

WHEN THE BOMBS FELL on Pearl Harbor on December 7, 1941, one phase of economic expansion closed. New ones opened.

On that day, 50,350,000 were employed in the country's labor force. The national income for the year was $103,834,000,000. There were already 1,470,000 in the armed forces.

In 1944, the year the European continent was invaded by the Allies, the national income rose to $182,800,000,000 and the armed forces were near their peak of 11,280,000.

Behind these statistics lay a world of challenge to government, business, labor — to all people. It was a challenge to the accounting profession.

Soon after Pearl Harbor, business began to face the handicaps of material and labor shortages, and a maze of other difficulties. Cost accounting became a major question. Production contracts, interim contracts and the keeping and administering of government records called for rapid handling.

Companies which had turned out typewriters geared their production to machine guns. Watchmakers made time-fuzes. All industry turned to with a common purpose.

There were other factors. Taxation for war needs was a burden, both as a levy and as an administrative problem. The accounting profession was called on to help plan, direct and supervise. Inventory control was complicated. New labor regulations were issued to control wages, hours, overtime and the training of labor for new jobs.

Plants which went ahead on retooling, expansion of facilities and training of new labor wanted, naturally, to be reimbursed. What if the manufacturer also produced goods in part of the plant for civilian use? What about wage and salary allocations? Factory costs were aggravated by delays in getting into production.

It was part of the accountants' job to interpret regulations, to advise and help guide business through the maze of accounting problems, to do their part of the job fairly and impartially, for the protection and welfare not only of the manufacturer but also of the government.

The American Institute of Accountants established committees and task forces at the outset to work with the Treasury Department, War Production Board, the Armed Services and other governmental bodies.

The task forces acted as consultants and observers, giving of their knowledge and experience. Contracts required that accounting methods conform to generally accepted accounting standards and many public spirited accountants volunteered their time to see that accounting methods were properly established and carried out.

The profession had its own internal and professional problems, too. These included technical questions on accounting, auditing, disbursing, cost accounting, cost analysis and problems of procedure and standards.

Reports to stockholders presented a new problem. Explanations and notes were greatly expanded and financial data was amplified, but there was the ever-present problem of how much to tell in financial figures so that vital information of value to the enemy would not be revealed.

Accounting firms had personnel problems. Younger men went into uniform. Older men, too. Many went to Washington to work in responsible positions with and for various government bodies.

Women played an important part. When the firms began to lose their younger men to the armed forces, they had to look for replacements. Many women who had been in bookkeeping positions of responsibility accepted staff positions where they gained great respect for their efforts and ability.

Accountants were in a position to clarify and simplify the vital job of channeling into government agencies the data needed to administer the war program and, as no business was allowed to exist that did not contribute to the war effort, practically every accountant in the country was directly or indirectly concerned with some part of the day to day operation.

By 1943, some of them were beginning to plan for the return to peacetime production. Reconversion was recognized as presenting a problem that had to be solved when the time came in order to prevent social and economic upheaval.

This was a cooperative effort. Aid came from many sources: from the accountants working in private business, without whose aid the public accountant could not have been successful, and from many organizations — the National Association of Cost Accountants, the Comptroller's Institute of America, the Institute of Internal Auditors and the American Accounting Association. And accountants in government agencies helped to smooth and simplify the many problems.

In 1943, the American Institute of Accountants started to study the reconversion and postwar problems of business. Return of young accountants after the war was anticipated; a committee developed a refresher course. Another committee began to study ways and means of attracting, selecting, evaluating and training prospective accountants. Other committees devoted attention to technical problems that were expected to arise.

With the invasion of France in June of 1944, the war moved ahead swiftly. Confidence rode high. Production was at flood tide. The problems did not lessen, but many seemed simpler. F. W. Lafrentz & Co., like all accounting firms, felt the pressure of the times. The burden of work fell on the partners. Even at that, many of the firm's partners found time to work on public service projects and professional committees. J. Arthur Marvin, for one, served as acting president in 1941, and president of the New York State Society of Certified Public Accountants in 1942-1943.

In May of 1945, the fighting in Europe ended and, in August, the enemy in the Pacific capitulated. The rush to reconversion began.

But there were fresh problems born out of the war, added responsibilities. It would take the combined energies of government, labor, business — and accounting — to meet them.

The profession had gained much out of the war. It proved its capacity; it had gained full stature and recognition. It proved again its importance as an economic and social force.

POSTWAR HORIZONS

THE UNITED STATES had demonstrated an undreamed of capacity. The demands of President Roosevelt had been received at first as fantastic. The nation had not only met the goals but had exceeded them.

As the great feeling of peace spread, it was mixed with questions of wonder as to the future. The giant production machine could no longer be used for the purposes for which it had been built. The problem ahead was peace.

And it was not just a matter of changing direction. For when the war was done some of the old signposts were gone, and the world's economic pattern was no longer quite the same. The problem was not how to return to the past but how to meet the future.

Both business and government, as early as 1943, had recognized that the transition to peace would call for the greatest dexterity and handling. Many businesses established "Plans Boards" to study the steps to be taken in relation to the preparations being developed by the War Production Board, Office of Contract Settlement, Office of Price Administration and the Armed Services. Leaders of the American Institute of Accountants joined in this work, giving what time could be spared from the war effort to the consideration of problems which were to mean so much to so many people. None the less, the amount of time that could be spent was relatively small and the transition from war to peace brought economic problems in its wake.

A FOUR-PHASE JOB

Many of the problems faced by business when the war ended related to accounting or were directly concerned with accounting. They grouped themselves into four phases:

1. First there was an immediate job to do. Thousands of plants

received notice of contract cancellations. Great masses of employes had to be whittled down or reassigned. Production lines were filled with unfinished, semi-finished and almost finished products — and what was to be done with them? And what was to be done with the great inventories which had been built up? What about settlement with the government and with the sub-contractors? Here was a whole complex of problems which had to be handled not in terms of weeks or months, but often in a matter of hours.

2. There was, second, the problem of raising management's sights for full-fledged reconversion and the long pull ahead. There were questions of disposing of war plants and materials, re-tooling for new kinds of production, searching for raw materials.

3. The third phase of the problem directly affected the accounting profession itself. For in addition to helping management adjust to its short and long range problems, the profession had to consider questions of personnel, expansion of services, and the whole broad question as to which way the profession was to develop. These were business problems too, for the internal problems of the profession had to be considered in terms of the services which would have to be provided.

4. There was, also, the question of the great expansion in men's thinking which stemmed from the shock of the war. The concepts of One World thinking, the Marshall Plan, the United Nations, the shortening of lines of communications, atomic energy — all these were political and economic questions which had meaning every day to businessmen and to the professional accountants working with them.

HOW THE JOB WAS TACKLED

As for the immediate problems, they were intensely practical and tangible. Companies had to furnish hundreds of reasonably precise records and reports to Government agencies. Payroll records had to be analyzed and interpreted. Short range forecasts had to be made on questions of employment, earning, disposition of inventories and scores of other such knotty questions.

At every turn, management found itself confronted with some-

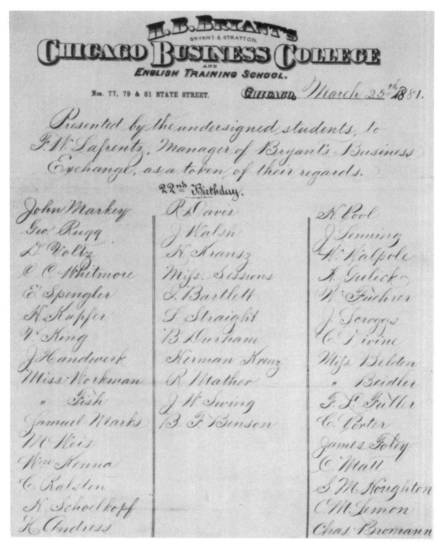

This testimonial was presented to F. W. Lafrentz on his 22nd birthday, March 25, 1881, by the students of Bryant & Stratton Business College.

thing it had to solve. Lights burned late in factories and plants throughout the nation as harassed business executives struggled to make adjustments which could very readily bring collapse and failure if not handled properly.

A great many of these problems of course were accounting problems or were related to accounting. And members of the profession, still shorthanded, had to work almost on a round-the-clock basis to help get the job done. These problems were common to all parts of the accounting profession, and the men of F. W. Lafrentz & Co. were in much the same position as the rest of the profession.

As time wore on, some practical aids to business developed. The excess profits tax was removed, providing a useful incentive for business, especially to some of the smaller firms which needed funds for retooling, acquisition of materials, and for the expansion of peacetime sales and distribution facilities.

Credit restrictions were eased. Consumers appeared to have substantial amounts of money to spend on both durable and non-durable goods — and these funds were backed up by a very substantial pent-up demand. Employment remained at a high level. These and related factors helped ease the situation as business and Government cooperated in a revamping of the economy.

Some of the factors in the picture were not wholly expected. The level of employment for example remained high, and the demand for capital and consumer goods seemed almost without limit. Many manufacturers who had anticipated a return to a "buyers' market" found that the combination of continued shortages and high demand served to maintain a "sellers' market."

DEPRECIATION AND COSTS

The accounting profession was deeply involved. There is no place here for even a summary of all the questions which the profession had to handle, but the important problem of depreciation may serve as an example of an economic and professional problem in which the accounting profession took the leadership.

In normal times, with a reasonably stable price level, it had always been possible to handle depreciation charges in a normal way. The manufacturer who had paid $100,000 for a plant could depreciate it over a period of say twenty years, at $5,000 a year, in the reasonable expectation that these charges would fairly represent the annual costs of using that plant.

But the postwar period was not normal. Because of much higher prices, the manufacturer with a plant that had cost $100,000 found that replacement costs on this kind of equipment were now several times as high as they had been. His plant might very well be worth $300,000 in terms of replacement costs, and it was — so the theory ran — a $300,000 facility that he was wearing out.

Question: was it right to continue to charge off depreciation on the basis of original cost? Or, should depreciation charges be increased, or accelerated or changed in some way to reflect the changed situation?

In some cases these depreciation problems were of the greatest import, and involved questions of millions of dollars. They were far from academic.

Opinion on how to handle the matter through the transitional years was far from unanimous. Some authorities felt that it would be proper to change traditional accounting methods, and in some fashion charge off depreciation on the basis of replacement costs. Some felt that this could be done by the use of an index figure of some sort, so that changes in depreciation charges could be related to an objective standard. Others felt that the only way to charge off the cost of depreciation was on the basis of original cost.

The confusion was reflected in the annual reports of some corporations. Some handled the problem on the basis of original cost, but some managements charged off costs which they felt more adequately reflected the situation before arriving at a determination of net income.

Naturally this whole question was one which concerned the accounting profession in a very immediate way.

One step in handling the problem was a survey made among business leaders by the American Institute of Accountants during the summer of 1948. The survey showed that, although opinion was still not unanimous — a great majority of responsible business leaders felt that original cost was still the best basis on which to determine the amount of depreciation to be charged against income.

Meanwhile, the Institute's Committee on Accounting Procedure worked arduously to try to determine the best solution. In the end the Institute's Committee promulgated its views. The statement held that business did face a real problem in handling depreciation charges, but that original cost still represented the best *yardstick*. The Committee recognized that it might often be necessary for prudent management to set aside extra reserves out of net income, but pointed out that it was proper to do so and to explain fully to stockholders and to the public why all of the funds reported as net earnings were not available for distribution.

Significantly the New York Stock Exchange issued a bulletin early in 1949 which supported the views taken by the accounting profession.

There were of course many other questions, and the depreciation problem is cited here only as an example.

SOME PROFESSIONAL SERVICES

While the profession was coping with these matters, its internal needs called for attention. Veterans needed retraining or refresher courses. There was work to be done with schools and colleges and other institutions where accounting was taught. New and better ways had to be found to select manpower, for the accounting profession was growing in numbers as well as in responsibilities, and it was clear that the quality of the services it could render would depend on the quality of the men who must render them.

The profession met these problems head on. All the facilities of the American Institute of Accountants were directed to the problems at hand.

Today the accounting profession is growing more rapidly than any other, and there are over 32,000 men and women who hold certificates as Certified Public Accountants in the forty-eight States and territories. More than ever before the skills and services of the profession are relied on by business, by Government agencies, by stockholders, by labor and by other segments of the public. The profession's wartime experiences and services have helped to increase public understanding of its functions.

Looking back it is clear that one result of the war was the opening of a whole new frontier of opportunity and responsibility.

In the field of Government for example there is much evidence that the contributions of the professional accountant are increasingly recognized. Members of the American Institute of Accountants have assisted in the studies of the House Committee on Appropriations. Professional leaders rendered assistance to the Hoover Commission in its studies of government structure. Others worked with the Armed Services in developing improved accounting tools for government contracts. The General Accounting Office has used the services of the profession, as have a wide variety of other agencies concerned with the question of how another mobilization would have to be handled in the event of another war. All along the line the profession has been able to serve the agencies of Government.

There are other groups who must depend on accounting because of its functions in the measurement of business progress: stockholders, banks, insurance companies and other credit grantors, members of other professions, courts and legislators.

Labor, too, increasingly uses the services of accounting, and the known independence and integrity of the professional practitioner is one of the factors which serves to lend validity to financial reports in which labor has a major interest.

The importance of these problems is one of the reasons why the profession has paid so much attention in recent years to the question of manpower selection. The profession has always tried to attract qualified and able young men and women to its ranks, but in 1943, when manpower shortages were acute, this effort was focussed sharply through the formation of the Committee on Selection of Personnel.

Under the supervision of this Committee, a "Personnel Selection Program" has been developed. Briefly, it provides a series of four tests which may be given to the student of accountancy or, in some cases, may be administered at the point of employment. Many thousands of these tests have been given and cooperation by colleges and institutions continues to grow. By early 1949 evidence had accumulated to show that the tests are of great value in telling the student, his teachers and his prospective employers something more than could be known before about his capacities, skills and orientation in the accounting field.

One of the great fields of concentration for the profession of course has been in the area of taxation. As was mentioned earlier, the determination of income has always been based on accounting concepts, and as the income tax has been spread more widely and more and more individual citizens have had to contend with problems in taxes. The profession has been active in helping taxpayers handle these problems and also in studying the whole concept of taxation to try to simplify this method of collecting revenue.

One of the most important areas of emphasis has been research. The American Institute of Accountants maintains an active Research Department, which is called on for everyday help by State Societies of Certified Public Accountants, by their Chapters, by their members and by a wide variety of governmental and business agencies for advice and counsel. The research studies made under the supervision of the Institute are regarded as authoritative.

The resolution of these many postwar problems and the guidance of postwar developments have been matters for the profession as a whole. Leadership had to spring out of the entire profession and not from any one group or firm. Members of the firm of F. W. Lafrentz & Co. have been proud to share in this work, recognizing that their burdens and contributions were not unique but reflections of the activities of all professional public accountants.

Today many of the firm's partners and staff members are active in the Institute, or in State Societies or Chapters of State Societies, giving their personal time and energies in an effort to contribute to the growth and advancement of the profession generally.

The Lafrentz organization stands on the threshold of its second half century. It has, in fifty years, passed through wars, depressions and boom times. It has faced the same growing pains and challenges faced by other accounting organizations.

There are today offices of the Lafrentz organization in 13 cities, and representatives in both England and Australia. There are 29 partners. Its activities in the accounting world are general and stretch into every field of business and commerce.

Fifty years is not a long time in terms of a profession whose roots go back for hundreds of years. But these have been fifty particularly exciting years. They have paralleled the growth of the accounting profession in this country and the enormous upsurge in business which began around the turn of the century. The men of F. W. Lafrentz & Co. find themselves far removed from the simple start on the ballroom balcony of the old Waldorf-Astoria Hotel.

The face of the world seems to change ever more rapidly. While there are some who may doubt the future, those who guide the affairs of F. W. Lafrentz & Co. believe that business and industry will expand; that this nation will play an increasingly important part in world affairs; that, as ways and means are worked out to establish a durable and lasting peace, the function of accounting will continue to expand in scope and importance.

The accounting profession has great responsibilities, not only to its own members, not only to its clients, but to society as a whole. It has not only technical skills and services to offer but the responsibility of helping to provide the means to bring about a better understanding among all the peoples of all the nations in the world.

F. W. Lafrentz & Co., at the end of one half century and the beginning of another, welcomes the opportunity to share in the exploration and development of these new frontiers.

IN ADDITION TO THOSE WHO ARE NOW PARTNERS in F. W. Lafrentz & Co., many contributions were made in years past by men who have passed on. They deserve a tribute from all who are carrying on the work of the firm today. Among these pioneers were:

C. B. Bidwell, of Atlanta; R. M. Coulbourn, of Baltimore; Fred E. Chamberlin, of Cleveland; Col. Lucien J. Moret, of New Orleans; E. P. Bergeron, H. A. Charlton, Theodore Cocheu, Jr., Charles W. Goetchius, Charles S. McCulloh and F. W. Rood of New York; Thomas P. Howard, Charles A. Peple and Allan Talbot of Richmond; and C. R. Cranmer of Washington, D. C.

A PROFESSION IS MEN

THE AUTHORITIES AGREE: that form of activity which we call a profession is marked by the subordination of gain to public service, by the observance of codes of ethics, by formal training, by the examination of candidates for admission, by the development and constant advancement of better methods for ministering to the needs of people.

The important word is *people*. It is people who have the needs, and people who must fulfill them. This is why, in the long development of the accounting profession, the emphasis has been on men, not on things; on human skills, not on mechanical procedures; on practical, every-day problems, not on theory. It has always been this way, and must be. There is a solid core of science and art, knowledge and methods, technical tools and forms. And men do the work.

In meeting the problems of the day's work, men seem to function best in organizations. It is organization which lends sharpness to the human skills. Eleven men wandering across a college campus have only their individual strengths; put together as a football team, they find extra strength and power in an extra factor: organization. There *are* times, in human equations, when the whole is greater than the sum of its parts: This is when the elements are organized, their energies harnessed for a common goal.

An emphasis on men, and on organization, was an essential part of F. W. Lafrentz's thinking at the start, as it continues to be. And since the partnership was first organized, each step on its expansion has been tested against the yardstick of utility and the principles of administration. For an organization of accountants must be geared to provide service, and this principle has guided and controlled the training of personnel for the firm, the admission of new partners and the creation of offices in key cities.

It seems appropriate, then, to say something of the men in many parts of the country who, as partners, conduct and guide the affairs of the company.

Since its founding in 1899 as The American Audit Company, F. W. Lafrentz & Co. has established offices in thirteen major cities in the United States. Four of these offices are located on the East Coast, three in the South, two in the industrial Mid-West and four on the West Coast. In addition to these offices, the firm maintains representation in London, England, and in Melbourne, Australia.

All told there are twenty-nine partners, including F. W. Lafrentz. Nine partners are in New York, four in San Francisco and three each in Baltimore and Richmond. There are two partners in Cleveland and two in Los Angeles, and one partner in Atlanta, Boston, Chicago, New Orleans, Oakland and Seattle.

The following pages give a brief biographical sketch of each of the firm's partners, telling something of their background, training and experience, and in which office each one is carrying on his work.

FOREIGN REPRESENTATION

LONDON • F. W. Lafrentz & Co. has been represented in London for over forty years by Martin, Farlow & Company. This firm was founded in the early 1880's by Sir James Martin and Arthur R. King-Farlow. Both gentlemen died in 1935. The present principals are Roland King-Farlow, son of the founder, Leonard R. Treen, and William G. Strachan, who were admitted to partnership in 1931 upon retirement of the founders, and Alan S. Hitchings who was admitted in 1942.

MELBOURNE • A. S. Bloomfield & Company have represented F. W. Lafrentz & Co. in Australia since 1938. The firm was founded by A. S. Bloomfield forty-nine years ago and was conducted as a partnership with G. B. Dicker until Mr. Bloomfield's retirement October 1, 1948. The present partnership is composed of Mr. Dicker and A. R. Pitts.

HILARY H. GARDNER ATLANTA

Hilary H. Gardner was born in Adairsville, Georgia. In 1909 he moved to Atlanta, where he took courses in business administration at the Georgia Institute of Technology, graduating in 1917. Mr. Gardner joined the Lafrentz organization on January 10, 1916 and, in 1925, succeeded the late C. B. Bidwell who had established the office in 1900. He was admitted to partnership on January 1, 1926. Mr. Gardner received his Georgia CPA certificate in 1925, and is a member of the American Institute of Accountants, Georgia Society of Certified Public Accountants and the National Association of Cost Accountants.

ALONZO LEE MILES BALTIMORE

The Baltimore office, established in 1906, was for many years managed by the late R. M. Coulbourn. Upon his retirement in 1928, Alonzo Lee Miles merged his practice with that of F. W. Lafrentz & Co. at which time he was admitted to partnership. Mr. Miles was born in Cambridge, Maryland, and began his accounting career with Haskins & Sells in 1917. He established his own practice two years later. He received his North Carolina CPA certificate in 1922, and his Maryland certificate in 1927. He is a member of the American Institute of Accountants, Maryland Society of Certified Public Accountants and the National Association of Cost Accountants.

JOSEPH A. NAEGELE BALTIMORE-WASHINGTON

Joseph A. Naegele, resident manager of the Washington office since 1941 and a partner in the Baltimore office since 1944, was born in Baltimore County, Maryland. He studied accounting at the University of Maryland School of Commerce, graduating in 1926. When Mr. Miles merged his practice with that of F. W. Lafrentz & Co., Mr. Naegele – then an associate of Mr. Miles – continued with the firm. He is a member of the American Institute of Accountants, Maryland Society of Certified Public Accountants and the National Association of Cost Accountants. The Washington office, established in 1903, was, for many years, in charge of the late C. R. Cranmer.

WILLIAM C. FRASER BALTIMORE

William C. Fraser was born in Ruxton, Maryland. After attending Baltimore Polytechnic Institute he entered on a career in banking which lasted sixteen years. During this period he studied accounting, commercial law and business administration at Johns Hopkins University. He joined F. W. Lafrentz & Co. on October 31, 1936, and was admitted to partnership October 1, 1944. Mr. Fraser received his District of Columbia CPA certificate in 1942, and his Maryland CPA certificate in 1945. He is a member of the American Institute of Accountants.

47 □

James W. Hall — Boston

Established in 1901, the Boston office has been managed continuously by James W. Hall since 1906, three years after he joined the Lafrentz organization. Mr. Hall is a native of Scotland. He studied at Gordons College and served as an audit clerk in London and Liverpool before coming to the United States in 1896. He has been a partner in F. W. Lafrentz & Co. since January 1, 1923. Mr. Hall took the first CPA examination held in Massachusetts and holds certificate No. 16. He is a member of the American Institute of Accountants and the Massachusetts Society of Certified Public Accountants.

Rollin M. Hickey — Chicago

Rollin M. Hickey, a native of Reedsburg, Wisconsin, has been in charge of the Chicago office since January 1, 1928, when he succeeded J. Arthur Marvin, now a partner in New York. Mr. Hickey joined F. W. Lafrentz & Co. December 10, 1923, not long after graduating from the University of Wisconsin. He was admitted to partnership January 1, 1929. He received his Illinois CPA certificate in 1926 and his Iowa certificate in 1944. He is a member of the American Institute of Accountants and the Illinois Society of Certified Public Accountants. The Chicago office opened in 1901. For many years it was under the direction of the late Francis R. Roberts.

Neal N. Scovill — Cleveland

Born in Cleveland, Neal N. Scovill studied accounting at Pace Institute (now Pace College), and worked as a cost accountant for several Cleveland manufacturing concerns, including The Hill Clutch Company, before joining the staff of Haskins & Sells in 1917. Five years later he resigned as Supervising Accountant to enter the partnership of Patton, Chamberlin & Scovill. On October 1, 1930, he and the late Fred E. Chamberlin were admitted to partnership in the Lafrentz organization. The Cleveland office was established in 1918.

William R. Gerlach — Cleveland

William R. Gerlach is a native of Cleveland. He attended Fenn College and in 1922 received his Ohio CPA certificate. On January 1, 1924, he joined the staff of F. W. Lafrentz & Co. He was admitted to partnership October 1, 1943. A graduate of John Marshall Law School in 1927, he was admitted to practice before the Ohio Bar in the same year. He was an instructor of law and accounting at Wilcox College of Commerce from 1928 to 1930, and is a member of the American Institute of Accountants and the Ohio Society of Certified Public Accountants.

WALTER K. MITCHELL — LOS ANGELES

Born in Griffin, Georgia, Walter K. Mitchell went to California in 1913, studied law at the University of California and, in 1919, established his own accounting practice. In 1927 he joined Fred E. Bullock and Harold A. Kellogg of San Francisco in forming Bullock, Kellogg & Mitchell, which merged with F. W. Lafrentz & Co., January 1, 1929. All three principals were admitted to partnership. Mr. Mitchell received his Georgia CPA certificate in 1910 and his California certificate in 1920. He is a member of the Bar of the United States Supreme Court, and a member of the American Institute of Accountants and the California Society of Certified Public Accountants.

A. DUDLEY BENSON — LOS ANGELES

A. Dudley Benson was born in England. He came to the United States in 1926 and settled in Los Angeles. He was on the staff of Price, Waterhouse & Co. for several years and, after accounting liaison work with the government during World War II, established his own practice in 1944 under the name of Benson & Co. This was merged with F. W. Lafrentz & Co. on February 1, 1947, at which time he was admitted to partnership. He received his California CPA certificate in 1936. Mr. Benson is a member of the American Institute of Accountants and the California Society of Certified Public Accountants.

THOMAS A. WILLIAMS — NEW ORLEANS

The New Orleans office was established in 1904. On November 1, 1928, Thomas A. Williams and his partner, the late Colonel Lucien J. Moret, merged their practice with that of F. W. Lafrentz & Co., and were admitted to partnership. Mr. Williams is a native of New Orleans and a graduate of Tulane University School of Business Administration and the Loyola University School of Law. He established his own practice in 1922, and received his Louisiana CPA certificate in 1923. He is a member of the American Institute of Accountants, Louisiana Society of Certified Public Accountants and the National Association of Cost Accountants.

GEORGE W. BREDEMEYER — NEW YORK

George W. Bredemeyer was born in New York City. He studied at Columbia University and is a graduate of Pace Institute (now Pace College). He began his accounting career with the firm of Ernst & Ernst. He joined the staff of F. W. Lafrentz & Co. on November 15, 1921, and was admitted to partnership on October 1, 1941. Mr. Bredemeyer received his New York CPA certificate in 1934, and is a member of the American Institute of Accountants and New York State Society of Certified Public Accountants.

Arthur F. Lafrentz — New York

Arthur F. Lafrentz was born in Cheyenne, Wyoming, and graduated from the Brooklyn Polytechnic Preparatory School. He joined the Lafrentz organization in 1904 as an office boy and was admitted to partnership on January 1, 1923. He received his New York State CPA certificate in 1922. Mr. Lafrentz is also President of the American Surety Company and of three of its subsidiaries and first vice-president of another. He is a member of the American Institute of Accountants, New York State Society of CPA's, Connecticut Society of CPA's, the Insurance Institute of America, and is a vice-president of the Chamber of Commerce of the State of New York.

J. Arthur Marvin — New York

J. Arthur Marvin was born in New York City. He went to Richmond, Virginia, in 1907 and joined the staff of the Richmond office in January 1914. He was appointed resident manager of the Chicago office on May 1, 1921 and was admitted to partnership in 1923. He transferred to the New York Office January 1, 1928. He received his Virginia CPA certificate in 1917 and his New York State certificate in 1925, and holds certificates from several other states. He is a member of the American Institute of Accountants, Virginia Society of Public Accountants, Illinois Society of CPA's, New York State Society of CPA's and the National Association of Cost Accountants.

Melvin D. Moersh — New York

Melvin D. Moersh was born in Cleveland and is a graduate of the University of Michigan. He joined the staff of A. G. Potter & Co., a Cleveland firm of public accountants, which merged its practice with that of F. W. Lafrentz & Co. in 1924. He became resident manager in 1928 and, two years later, transferred to New York where he was admitted to partnership in 1941. Mr. Moersh received his New York State CPA certificate in 1937. He is a member of the American Institute of Accountants, New York State Society of Certified Public Accountants and the Institute of Internal Auditors.

Harry M. Rice — New York

Harry M. Rice was born in Riceville, Pennsylvania and began his accounting career in Pittsburgh. He became southern manager for the Audit Company of New York and, while in Atlanta, helped organize the State Board of Accountancy and the establishment of a CPA law. He holds Georgia certificate No. 4, and, also, certificates in other states. He later served as Commissioner of Accounts for the City of New York under Mayor Gaynor and joined the Lafrentz organization in 1913. A partner since January 1, 1923, he is a 33 degree Mason and a member of the Royal Order of Scotland and a Knight of the Red Cross of Constantine.

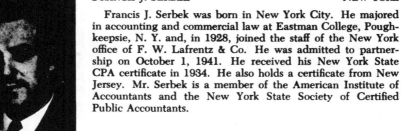

FRANCIS J. SERBEK   NEW YORK

Francis J. Serbek was born in New York City. He majored in accounting and commercial law at Eastman College, Poughkeepsie, N. Y. and, in 1928, joined the staff of the New York office of F. W. Lafrentz & Co. He was admitted to partnership on October 1, 1941. He received his New York State CPA certificate in 1934. He also holds a certificate from New Jersey. Mr. Serbek is a member of the American Institute of Accountants and the New York State Society of Certified Public Accountants.

PETER C. WIEGAND   NEW YORK

Peter C. Wiegand was born in New York City. He began his accounting career with Patterson, Teele & Dennis, resigning twelve years later to become executive accountant for a large business concern. In December 1926, he joined the staff of F. W. Lafrentz & Co. and on January 1, 1930 was admitted to partnership. Mr. Wiegand received his New York State CPA certificate in 1905. He also holds a certificate from New Jersey. He is a member of the American Institute of Accountants, New York State Society of Certified Public Accountants and the New Jersey Society of Certified Public Accountants.

JAMES H. WREN   NEW YORK

James H. Wren was born in Lynchburg, Virginia, and attended Emory and Henry College. He practiced public accounting in Virginia and in New York City and joined the staff of F. W. Lafrentz & Co. on November 1, 1934. He studied at New York University, Columbia University and at Pace Institute (now Pace College). In 1915 he received his Virginia CPA certificate and, in 1933, his New York State certificate. Mr. Wren was admitted to partnership October 1, 1941. He is a member of the American Institute of Accountants, New York State Society of Certified Public Accountants and the National Association of Cost Accountants.

GEORGE R. GEDDY   RICHMOND

George R. Geddy, partner in charge of the Richmond office since 1928, was born in James City County, Virginia. He attended Eastman Business College at Poughkeepsie, N. Y., and was employed by the Life Insurance Company of Virginia prior to joining the Richmond office staff on September 1, 1920. Mr. Geddy was admitted to partnership on July 1, 1926 and succeeded Allan Talbot as partner in charge upon his resignation. He received his Virginia CPA certificate in 1925 and is a member of the American Institute of Accountants and the Virginia Society of Public Accountants. The Richmond office was established in 1907.

STUART D. WALDEN — RICHMOND

Stuart D. Walden was born in Lynchburg, Virginia, and moved to Richmond at an early age. He attended Virginia Mechanics Institute, College of William and Mary extension division and the University of Richmond School of Business Administration. He joined the staff of F. W. Lafrentz & Co. on September 6, 1920, and was admitted to partnership on October 1, 1947. Mr. Walden received his Virginia CPA certificate in November 1934. He is a member of the American Institute of Accountants and the Virginia Society of Public Accountants.

ROBERT W. ZIMMERMAN, JR. — RICHMOND

Robert W. Zimmerman, Jr., was born in New York City and is a graduate of the University of Virginia. He entered public accounting in 1939 and joined the staff of F. W. Lafrentz & Co. in New York on April 1, 1940. He became a member of the Richmond office staff in 1945. He was admitted to partnership on October 1, 1947. Mr. Zimmerman received his New York State CPA certificate in 1943 and his Virginia certificate in 1947. He is a member of the American Institute of Accountants, Virginia Society of Public Accountants and the National Association of Cost Accountants.

HAROLD A. KELLOGG — SAN FRANCISCO

Harold A. Kellogg was born in San Francisco. He became Assistant Superintendent of Accounts for the California State Board of Control and, on May 1, 1921, he formed a partnership with Fred D. Bullock in the practice of public accounting. Walter K. Mitchell merged his practice in Los Angeles with theirs in 1927 and, on January 1, 1929, Bullock, Kellogg & Mitchell merged its practice with that of F. W. Lafrentz & Co. All three principals were admitted to partnership. Mr. Kellogg received his California CPA certificate in 1919, and is a member of the American Institute of Accountants and the California Society of Certified Public Accountants.

ROBERT H. PERRY — OAKLAND

Robert H. Perry was born in Iroquois County, Illinois, attended business college and studied law at Wesleyan University, Bloomington, Illinois. He began his career in Bloomington and entered public accounting in San Francisco in 1919. He established his own practice in Oakland in 1922 and merged it with that of F. W. Lafrentz & Co. on January 1, 1930, and was admitted to partnership in the San Francisco and Oakland offices in charge of the Oakland office. He received his California CPA certificate in 1924 and is a member of the American Institute of Accountants and the California Society of Certified Public Accountants.

ROBERT M. GANE   SAN FRANCISCO

Robert M. Gane was born in Cleveland. He settled in San Francisco in 1920 and studied at the San Francisco Institute of Accountancy. In March 1928, he received his California CPA certificate, then taught mathematics and accountancy for two years. He established his own accounting practice in 1930 and in 1938 merged it with F. W. Lafrentz & Co. and became a partner in that year. Mr. Gane is a member of the American Institute of Accountants, California Society of Certified Public Accountants and the National Association of Cost Accountants.

LEONARD M. TICE   SAN FRANCISCO

Leonard M. Tice was born in San Joaquin County, California. He studied at the San Francisco Institute of Accounting, Golden Gate College and the University of California Extension School In 1923 he joined the staff of Bullock & Kellogg, predecessor firm of F. W. Lafrentz & Co. in California. He is a certified public accountant in California and was admitted to partnership in October 1, 1947. He is a member of the American Institute of Accountants and the California Society of Certified Public Accountants.

FRED D. BULLOCK   SAN FRANCISCO

Fred D. Bullock was born in Hayward, California. He studied at Pace Institute (now Pace College) in New York City and established his own accounting practice in 1919. Harold A. Kellogg joined him as a partner in May 1921 and, on September 1, 1927, Walter K. Mitchell merged his practice in Los Angeles with theirs. Bullock, Kellogg & Mitchell merged its practice with F. W. Lafrentz & Co. on January 1, 1929. Mr. Bullock received his California CPA certificate in 1918 and is a member of the American Institute of Accountants and the California Society of Certified Public Accountants. In recent years he has withdrawn his more active participation in the firm but continues to serve in a consulting capacity.

ARNE S. HANSEN   SEATTLE

Arne S. Hansen was born in Gilbert, Iowa. He moved to the west at an early age and, after studying at Pacific Lutheran Academy, began his accounting career in 1907. He soon established Arne S. Hansen & Co. He was appointed the representative of F. W. Lafrentz & Co. in 1930 and, in 1935, a partnership was formed with Mr. Hansen to handle the expanding activities of the firm's clients in the Pacific-Northwest. Mr. Hansen obtained his Washington CPA certificate in December 1913. He is a member of the American Institute of Accountants and the Washington Society of Certified Public Accountants.

53 ☐

ACCOUNTING HISTORY AND THOUGHT

An Empirical Study of Financial Disclosure by
Swedish Companies.
  T. E. Cooke

Accountability of Local Authorities in
England and Wales, 1831–1935.
  Edited by Malcolm Coombs and J. R. Edwards

Accounting Methodology and the
Work of R. J. Chambers
  Michael Gaffikin

Schmalenbach's *Dynamic Accounting* and
Price-Level Adjustments.
An Economic Consequences Explanation
  O. Finley Graves, Graeme Dean, and Frank Clarke

An Analysis of the Early Record Keeping in the
Du Pont Company, 1800–1818.
  Roxanne Therese Johnson

The Closure of the Accounting Profession
  Edited by T. A. Lee

Shareholder Use and Understanding of
Financial Information
  T. A. Lee and D. P. Tweedie

The Selected Writings of Maurice Moonitz
  Maurice Moonitz

Methodology and Method in History
A Bibliography
  Edited by Lee D. Parker and O. Finley Graves

Accounting in Australia
Historical Essays
  Edited by Robert H. Parker

*Academy of Accounting Historians Classics Series

Garland publishes books on all aspects of the accounting profession; for a
complete list of titles please contact the publisher.